How do you like our book?

We would really appreciate you leaving us a review.

Other Picture Books:

For other fun Picture Books by Kampelstone, simply search for:

Kampelstone Picture Books

Interesting facts about wolves

- 'Canis Lupus' is Latin for Gray Wolf, the most common type of wolf..

- Some say that 'Canis Rufus', Latin for Red Wolf, is to be a cross-breed between a Gray Wolf and coyote.

- 'Canis Simensis', the Ethiopian Wolf, lives in isolated mountain areas in the Ethiopian highlands.

- Many subspecies of wolves have become extinct, while the remaining wolves are in a vulnerable state.

- To help bring the species back from the brink, wolves are being reintroduced into the wild in Eastern Europe and the USA.

- Wolves live in packs of up to 20.

- A wolf can grow to be 5ft (1.5 meters) long and stand 3ft (.9 meters) high.

- Gray wolves can often grow to over 175 lb (80 kg).

- A female wolf can have as many as six pups.

- While hunting, wolves prefer large prey such as deer or boar but will certainly take a rabbit or a lamb if that is what is available.

- A wolf can eat up ro 22 lb (10 kg) of meat in one meal.

- Wolves are estimated to live up to 13 years old.

- Their long muzzle ends with a hyper sensitive nose, which is one hundred times better than a human's.

- Pack alphas, the male and female pack leaders, are usually the only couple to mate. At the other end of the spectrum, there will always be omega males and females; the low ones in the social ranking. Omegas never mate.

- Female wolves, called bitches, live in dens underground during Spring so that they can bear and take care of their pups who are born deaf and blind.

- The entire pack assists in caring for the new pups.

- A wolf's howl is a method of communication that is the loudest when in harmony with others. A single wolf howl can be heard up to 10km.

- A wolf's hearing is twenty times better than a human's.

- Wolves are able to travel 120 miles (200 km) within one full day.

- In Roman mythology, Romulus and Remus were raised by wolves.

- The werewolf legend originated in an ancient Greek myth where King Lycaon of Arcadia insulted Zeus so Zeus turned King Lycaon into a wolf. Additionally, Herodotus wrote that the Neuri people living in the north-east of Scythia were all transformed into wolves every year for several days, and then changed back to their human shape.

- In native American cultures, the wolf is believed to be a pathfinder and teacher.

- Wolves have a characteristic penetrating and hauntingly beautiful howl. This howl acts as a communication tool, between lone wolves and their pack or just between packs.

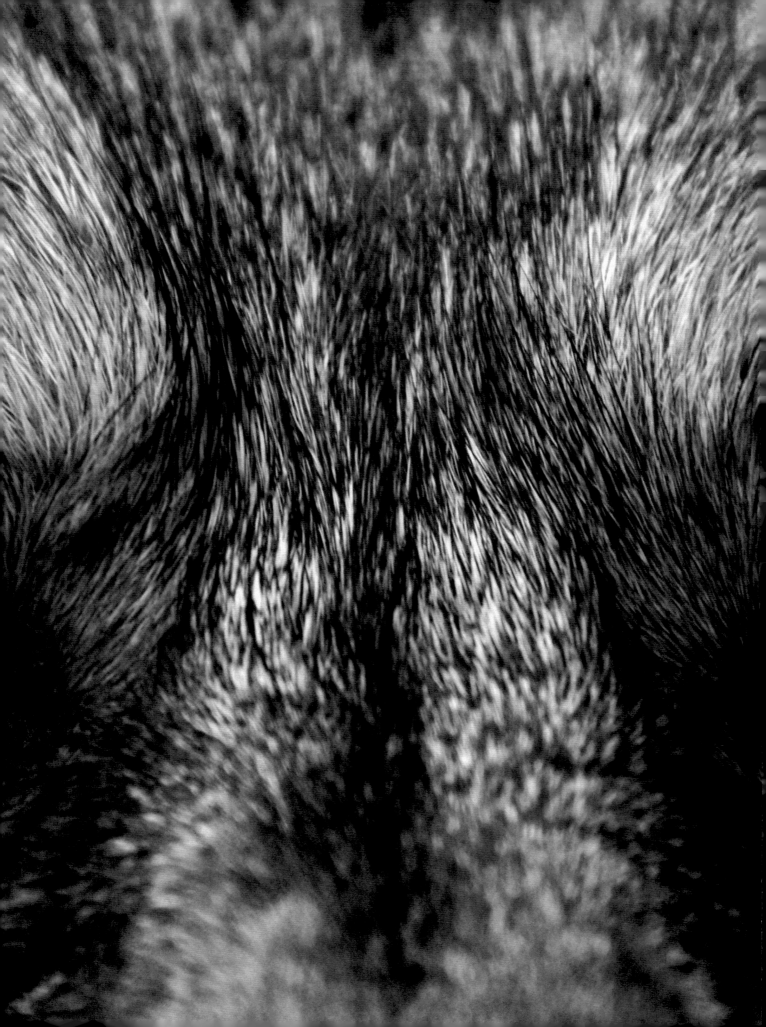

efae902d-7b5e-4cba-a96c-ef32f7741a04R01